EAST LANCASHIRE COACHBUILDERS

DAVID BARROW

AMBERLEY

George Alcock (left) and Arthur Danson (right) in front of the first ELCB tramcar for Blackpool Transport in June 1984.

First published 2021

Amberley Publishing
The Hill, Stroud
Gloucestershire, GL5 4EP

www.amberley-books.com

Copyright © David Barrow, 2021

The right of David Barrow to be identified as the Author of this work has been asserted in accordance with the Copyrights, Designs and Patents Act 1988.

ISBN 978 1 3981 0227 9 (print)
ISBN 978 1 3981 0228 6 (ebook)

British Library Cataloguing in Publication Data.
A catalogue record for this book is available from the British Library.

Typesetting by SJmagic DESIGN SERVICES, India.
Printed in the UK.

Introduction

East Lancashire Coachbuilders was first registered as a viable company on 27 October 1934, with four directors all residing in around Blackburn in Lancashire. At the end of 1935 one of the directors resigned, followed by two more in the summer of 1937. This left just one director Walter Smith. Enter Alfred Alcock and George Danson. Both were employed by Massey Brothers in Wigan, also in Lancashire. Alfred was General Manager, while George was works foreman.

In 1937 both Alcock and Danson were restless for a change and took the decision to go it alone and start their own company. They choose Bolton as an ideal place, but finding suitable premises at an affordable rent proved impossible. So they turned their attention to Blackburn. Reaching an agreement with Walter Smith, they formed a new company based on his premises at Brookhouse Mill on Whalley New Road, which incidentally dated back to 1884 as a former weaving shed. The reconstituted company East Lancashire Coachbuilders Ltd was formed on 9 May 1938 with four directors: Walter Smith, his wife Lilian, Alfred Alcock and George Danson.

Their first order came from Bolton Corporation Transport for ten double-deck bodies mounted on Leyland chassis. This order was completed by the end of 1938. The company's customer base expanded over the following years, and especially after the end of the Second World War. When Leyland ceased building bus bodywork in 1954 East Lancs was able to capitalise on this gap in the market, supplying bodywork to the majority of Lancashire municipals, and to a number of south coast operators. Southdown, probably the largest of all south coast operators, stated that of all double-deck bodywork supplied to them in the early 1950s the East Lancs examples stood out among the rest as a quality product.

In 1958 Walter Smith sadly died and his shares in the company were sold to a third party, simply because the Danson family was not prepared to pay what the family of Walter Smith required. In 1963 all shares in the company were sold to Bishopgate Nominees Ltd. At around this time both Alcock's and Danson's two sons, George and Arthur, both became directors. Alfred Alcock retired in 1966 and George Danson in 1984.

In 1963 a subsidiary was set up in Sheffield by the name of Neepsend to build bodywork to East Lancs drawings and procedures. Production came to an end in Sheffield in the winter of 1968, and approximately 200 complete single- and double-deck buses were produced over a five-year period.

In 1970 the Whalley New Road factory suffered a catastrophic fire, which destroyed a large section of the main building. Rebuilding work commenced some two months later, and the company was back in full production in a little over twelve months.

In 1990 Arthur Danson took early retirement, and sadly died in 1995. Chris Clarke, who was an engineering consultant with the Drawlane Group, was appointed Chief Executive for East Lancs in January 1992 following the retirement of George Alcock. George died in 2018 at the age of eighty-three. Chris was instrumental in the development of the National Greenway project and the introduction with Scania of the OmniDekka. Chris passed away in 2002 at the age of just fifty-eight.

In 1994 the decision was made to move production 1 mile across town to the Whitebirk Industrial Estate. The new factory was 50 per cent larger than the old site, and there they remained until the end.

Owners over the years have been, in addition to those mentioned, Cravens, John Brown plc, Trafalgar House and the Drawlane Group. In August 2007 the East Lancashire Coachbuilders name was no more after the company was taken over by the Darwen Group. The events that followed are beyond the scope of this book.

Throughout my long association with the company four personalities stand out above the rest: Arthur Danson, George Alcock and the two works managers, John Bufton and Brian Duxbury. Sadly all four are no longer with us. I can still hear Brian shouting at me across the factory floor 'You shouldn't be in here', only to find in later years he was my first port of call if I needed anything.

Many Saturday mornings were spent in Arthur's upstairs office discussing the new orders he had secured that week, and on the odd occasion he would invite me to accompany him to a handing over ceremony (Kingston upon Hull springs to mind). It was there that I first met Ted Reid, another person who I would spend many a happy hour in the company of.

The majority of the photographs in this book have never been published and come from my extensive collection. However, I am indebted to Peter Graham for giving me permission to include the photographs of Wally Talbot, who was the official East Lancs photographer for over thirty years. Others are G. Ashton, A. J. Douglas, W. J. Haynes, Andrew Jarosz, Martin Yates, Jeff Johnson, Malcolm King, Robin Hannay, H. Rich, J. S. Cockshott, The Transport Library and the Omnibus Society and to the others I have been unable to trace. I am also indebted to John Gibson, and again Martin Yates for their extensive knowledge of production dates and numbers. Finally, also to a former work colleague, Wally Drinkwater, who first introduced me to Arthur Danson.

The first order received was from Bolton Corporation for ten double-deck bodies mounted on the Leyland TD5 chassis. All were built and in service by the end of 1938.

Two further orders were received in 1938 from Leigh and Chester. The Leigh example was again on a TD5 chassis, but built to low-bridge height. These two orders were also delivered in 1938.

Naturally Blackburn Corporation would become a regular customer, and in 1939 placed its first order with East Lancs for two double-decks mounted on AEC Regent I, seen here about to be delivered in Blackburn's fully lined out livery.

In 1942 they rebodied a 1930 Leyland TD1 for Eastbourne Corporation, another operator who was to become a repeat customer. Note the wartime white edge markings.

In 1942 Southdown sent two Leyland TD2s to Blackburn for rebodying. Such was their satisfaction with what they received, that they sent buses for new bodywork every year until 1950. This one is a Leyland TD5.

Production got back in full swing in 1946/7, and some early examples were three low-bridge Leyland PD1s for Leigh. They were built to a four-bay design with lower deck 'D' shaped windows.

This is another of Southdown's large batch of rebodies, this time on a TD4 chassis.

Numerically the first production Leyland PD2 chassis came off the line in June 1947, but it would be 1948 when it was finally bodied for Rawtenstall Corporation, becoming fleet number 11 (JTE 486).

These next two photographs show Rochdale Corporation Transport's first East Lancs bodywork of 1948 in the shape of seven AEC Regent IIIs. Their well-rounded design was constructed to the newly approved 8-foot width.

Rochdale AEC Regent III 207 (GDK 407).

Eastbourne Corporation became a loyal customer. This Leyland PD2/1 of 1948 is one of four supplied for the Willingdon village service, 25 (JK 9983).

The only new Crossley double-decks bodied by East Lancs were eight DD42/5 models for Eastbourne. 35 (JK 9992) is seen passing the town's railway station in the early 1960s.

Production was not confined to diesel engine buses, but also electric propulsion. Six of these BUT 9611Ts were supplied to Darlington in 1949. A number of trolleybuses were rebodied in the mid-1940s. Included was a batch of twenty-five for London Transport, which were damaged by enemy aircraft in 1940.

Burnley Colne and Nelson Joint Transport took four of these Leyland PD2/3s in 1949.

This Leyland PD1A, supplied to Accrington Corporation Transport in 1949, would give fifteen years' service to the east Lancashire town.

The Daimler CD650 was not a total success in terms of sales. Only twenty-four were built. It was fitted with a large 10.6-litre, six-cylinder engine, when the norm from AEC and Leyland was 9.6 or 9.8. Five were exported to Johannesburg, but the largest number, a total of six, went to Halifax Corporation and Joint Transport Committee in 1951. All six were withdrawn in 1962.

Nottingham City Transport was to become a regular customer, up to and beyond the demise of the ELCB name. The first bodywork to be ordered by Nottingham was four AEC Regal IIIs in 1951.

Six low-bridge AEC Regent IIIs were supplied to Huddersfield in 1952.

Guy Arabs became a popular choice in the Accrington fleet. Five mark IVs came in 1953.

When Leyland ceased to build bodywork Rawtenstall Corporation switched to East Lancs, taking four PD2/12s in 1953.

An export order was gained in 1954 for fifteen double-deck trolleybuses mounted on BUT chassis for Ceylon-based Colombo Municipal Transport. The first one is seen here ready for its twenty-day sea journey to Ceylon.

In 1967 Southend took its last front engine/rear entrance double-deckers. Originally they were to have Massey bodywork, but after takeover by Northern Counties, also in Wigan, they decided to go to East Lancs. 345 to 347 came at the end of 1967. 345(MHJ 345F) is here on Marine Parade.

Another PD2/12, this time for Burnley Colne & Nelson. 219 (DHG 219) was one of six delivered in 1955.

Bolton Corporation Transport Leyland Royal Tiger PSU1/14 fleet number 9 (GWH 516) was new in 1955. This was the first new East Lancs body on a new chassis supplied to Bolton.

Leigh Corporation low-bridge Leyland PD2/20 47 (WTE 21). It was fitted with the new style BMMO tin front. This was first introduced by Leyland in 1952.

Birkenhead took five Leyland PD2/12s in 1955. 333 (DCM 983) is seen ready for delivery.

Southdown's twenty-four PD2/12s of 1956/7 are fitted with their patented 'Eastlanco' single piece sliding door. 804 (RUF 204) is seen here in Southsea in 1967. The operator was heard to say upon delivery that these were a credit to the company for the quality of the finished product.

This Bradford trolleybus was a 1944 Karrier W belonging to Darlington. It was acquired by Bradford in 1958 and fitted with a new body.

The same bus is undergoing a tilt test at the Blackburn factory. George Danson is on the left of the photograph.

A 'tin front' Leyland PD2/20 new to Rawtenstall in 1955, 62 (VTJ 733) is seen in Accrington town centre when new on the Bacup to Accrington service.

A 1954 PD2/12 of Haslingden Corporation Transport department. 5 (TTB 302) was the only new bus ordered that year.

Hutchings and Cornelius of South Petherton, Somerset. This Dennis Loline was bought by H&C in June 1958 and sold in July 1973. This was the only bus ever built by ELCB for H&C.

After a gap of three years of buying no new buses, in 1958 only one new bus was received at Rawtenstall in the shape of a Leyland PSUC1/5, a forty-three-seat, front entrance single-decker.

In 1961 Accrington Corporation Transport took two Guy Wulfrunains. Intended as a front engine bus, Accrington had the only rear entrance Wulfrunian. They proved very unreliable and were withdrawn after just seven years. East Lancs only bodied five examples.

The Dennis Loline was basically a licence-built Bristol Lodekka. In 1958 Aldershot & District bought four with East Lancs bodywork. When Loline production ceased in 1966 A&D had built up a fleet of 120, but these are the only East Lancs examples.

Lancaster City Transport bought three of these Leyland PSUC1/3 in 1958, and two more came the following year.

Luton Corporation Transport took five of these low-bridge PD2/30s in 1960, and in the following years would also receive Dennis Lolines and Albion Lowlanders from East Lancs.

In 1958 Leyland introduced a new glass fibre full width front bonnet assembly, designed in conjunction with St Helens General Manager John Wake to improve the drivers nearside vision.

North Western Road Car at Stockport, Cheshire, took fifteen Dennis Lolines in 1960.

Leicester's first East Lancs bodywork arrived in 1960 in the shape of four 30-foot-long Leyland PD3/1s, and would become an important customer for the next thirty years.

The AEC Regent was a popular choice in the south of England. Both Eastbourne and Southampton would take Regent Vs. This is a 1962 example for Eastbourne.

Bolton divided their orders between East Lancs and MCW. One of the Blackburn examples is a fully fronted Leyland PD3A/2, new in 1962. It is pictured in Bury town centre on the 52 service between Bolton and Bury via Radcliffe.

Some of the company's first rear engine double-decks went to Warrington, mounted on Daimler Fleetlines. They took nine in 1963.

What was to become the standard ELCB double-deck design for the next twenty years first appeared on a Leyland Atlantean for Bolton, which was designed in conjunction with the then Bolton General Manager Ralph Bennett.

A bus from the same batch outside Bolton Town Hall in April 1963.

This Cardiff Guy Arab was built by Neepsend in Sheffield in 1964.

Another Neepsend product, this time a AEC Regent V for Southampton.

The first new double-deck for Rawtenstall in nine years came in 1964: four front entrance 30-foot-long Leyland PD3/4s.

Reading had eight of these AEC Reliances in 1964/5. They were constructed with larger than normal side windows.

Bury Corporation Transport's first ever bodywork from Blackburn came in April 1965. They took six on Daimler Fleetlines. Bury's previous double-decks had come from MCW and Alexander.

One of the same order in service in Tottington.

More Fleetlines for Warrington in 1965, which are similar to the Bury examples.

Maynes of Manchester took a Neepsend-bodied AEC Regent V in 1965.

Burnley Colne & Nelson Leyland PD2A/27 of 1965.

Huddersfield had this 30-foot-long front entrance Daimler CVG6 new in 1966.

Another Yorkshire operator to take East Lancs bodywork in the 1950s/60s was Bradford, on both AECs, Leylands and Daimlers. This is one of the latter.

In 1966 Leicester took ten AEC Renowns with rear entrance bodywork. The previous year they took three with front entrances. The Renown was a low-bridge chassis, fitted with high-bridge bodywork.

A 1966 Leyland PD2A/30 for Eastbourne Corporation Transport.

This Neepsend-bodied AEC Regent V of 1966 was part of an order for four built for Ipswich. It was withdrawn in 1986.

Bury Corporation Transport's previous single-deckers had been either Leyland or AEC, but in 1967 they went for the Daimler Fleetline.

Internal view of the single-deck Fleetline for Bury.

Stockport Corporation favoured front engine Leylands right up until the very end of production.
This rear entrance PD3/14 came in the spring of 1968.

Stockport Leyland PD3/14 MJA 891G has now been restored to its former glory.

Bury Corporation reverted back to front engine Leylands for their 1967 delivery. Four PD2/37 were obtained exclusively for service 23T to Bolton, which had a weight restriction on a railway bridge in Bolton town centre.

More Daimler Fleetlines came to Bury in 1968. 140 (HEN 540F) is seen outside Derby Hall.

These two Leyland Atlanteans are for two different customers. The one on the left is a PDR2/1 for Manchester Corporation, and the other is a PDR1A/1 for Bolton.

The Manchester example is one of twenty-four (twelve single door and twelve two door). The company won another order from Manchester, but because of the 1970 fire the order was given to Chas Roe in Leeds.

Bury's first two-door double-decks were three Leyland Atlanteans in revised livery. During the previous year Bury had standardised on the Daimler Fleetline.

The last front engine Leyland double-deck was ordered by Ramsbottom Urban District Council, but was delivered to SELNEC in November 1969. Now fully restored, it is seen at the East Lancs factory in 2004.

Ordered by Bury Corporation, the seven two-door Daimler Fleetlines of 1971 were painted in the SELNEC livery of orange and white, but with Bury green interiors.

Coventry 82 (YHP 482J) was one of a batch of eighteen Daimler Fleetlines new in 1971. All were transferred to the West Midlands PTE in April 1974.

Fifteen 33-foot-long Atlantean PDR2/1s were ordered by Bolton but delivered to SELNEC Northern in 1971.

An Eastbourne Leyland Atlantean on test in Blackburn in March 1972.

The first Dennis Dominator went to No. 10 Downing Street to meet the then Prime Minister James Callaghan to present an award to the Hestair Dennis Managing Director John Smith.

Dennis Dominator SHE 722S at the entrance to Downing Street in November 1978.

The National Greenway before and after conversion. Both are on London General Red Arrow services at Victoria station. A revised front and rear was designed in conjunction with Ray Stenning (Best Impressions) at the request of Keith Ludeman MD, St London General.

East Yorkshire embraced the National Greenway in 1982 for services in Scarborough.

Kentish Bus was another convert. One of the routes they would be seen on was the 227 Bromley–Beckenham–Crystal Palace.

This Crosville example, branded 'C' line, started life with Ribble Motor Services as Leyland National MK2 875 (LFR 875X).

The National Greenway project involved a complete strip down to a bare shell. At first all mechanical work was carried out by London Country (South West) in Reigate, and later on Blackburn Borough Transport's Intack depot. Newly remanufactured Gardner or Volvo engines replaced the Leyland units. A total of 178 were produced over a five-year period.

The first Scania Cityzens were thirteen for Northumbria Motor Services, part of British Bus. The first example is 381 (N381 NTY), photographed passing the former factory in January 1996.

East Lancs built three so-called coaches in 1975. Two were on the Leyland Leopard chassis, and the other one (photographed here) for Hyndburn on a Seddon RU. The two Leopards were later rebodied as service buses. Suffice to say it was not the success the company had hoped.

Maynes of Manchester took a total of eight Cityzens between 1996 and 2000. One of the first four, 2 (P102 HNC), is seen in Piccadilly Gardens on the 233 service to Carrbrook. In total eighty-six Scania Cityzens were sold between January 1996 and December 2000.

Fleet number 400 (NRR 400W), a Scania BR112DH, was only a demonstrator for a very short period before joining the fleet of Nottingham City Transport. NCT wanted to buy a further eighty, but the city council thought they should buy British. However, within five years NCT was buying from both Scania and Volvo in large numbers.

Some of Warrington Borough Council's last Leyland Atlanteans was five supplied in 1981. 20 (MEK 20W) is seen outside the factory ready for delivery.

Only six Dennis Falcon V double-decks were built – three by East Lancs and three by Northern Counties of Wigan. The East Lancs examples were two for Nottingham (above) and a demonstrator in 1981/2.

The Volvo Ailsa front engine double-deck chassis came on the market in 1973. When production came to an end in 1985, a total of 1,047 had been sold, both in the UK and for export. Out of that total East Lancs built only twenty-five, and for one customer, Tayside, in 1983.

In 1998 East Lancs secured an order to assemble thirty Dennis Trident three axle double-decks for Citybus in Hong Kong. The contract was undertaken for Duple-Metsec Ltd using their frames. The first one to be completed is seen in Blackburn town centre in May 1998.

The same bus in another part of Blackburn.

A Citybus parked at Southampton docks on 6 October 1998.

A total of four again at Southampton. Shipping time to Hong Kong was twenty-nine days.

Another Hong Kong-bound Dennis Trident about to be reversed onboard the Panama registered *Queen Ace* on 18 December 1998.

Onboard the *Queen Ace*, one East Lancs-built Trident in the company of three similar examples built at Caetano in Portugal.

Fleet number 2221 (HY2 758) entering Causeway Bay bus station on 9 February 1999.

Another contract for Duple Metsec was for three left-hand-drive Dennis Lances for Poland.

In 1997 two Spryte-bodied Dennis Dart SLFs were supplied to Leo Grech at Paramount Garages at Mosta in Malta. This one was six months old when photographed.

George Alcock stated that in his mind the two Leyland Olympians they built for London Buses 'London Liner' service to Eastbourne were the finest buses the company had ever built. At 11.4 metres long and 4.3 metres high, the luxury vehicles were fitted with a rear-mounted toilet and seventy Lazzarini seats. They were completed in July 1985.

Andrews of Sheffield, part of the Yorkshire Traction Group, took eleven Myllennium single-decks on the DAF SB220GS chassis in 2000. Used on the cross-city service 74, 1275 (W47 5 MKU) is parked close to the M1 Tinsley Viaduct.

SHEET 1 OF 2 SHEETS

DRG Nº R.V. 2263/2A

EAST LANCASHIRE COACHBUILDERS LTD

This is a sketch of the proposed final version of the Dodge minibus.

One of eight Dodge 50 series minibuses in-build for Newport on 16 May 1987. The Dodge had a 90 bhp Perkins four-cylinder turbo-charged diesel engines, coupled to a Torqueflite three-speed automatic gearbox.

Les Cars Rouge Paris took six left-hand-drive open-top 12-metre-long Volvo B10Ms in 1999 for sightseeing duties in the French capital.

A Gloucestershire Incident Command Unit built around a Dennis Dart chassis.

A view inside the factory, *c*. 1973. On the left is a Seddon RU for Accrington, 35 (OTF 376M), and on the right is Warrington Daimler Fleetline NED 313M.

In 1994 the company moved production to another area of Blackburn. The last bus to be completed in the old factory was a Leyland Olympian for Nottingham City Transport, 486 (L486 NTO). It carries an appropriate destination display as it exits the empty factory for the last time.

In 1992 Rossendale Transport had two thirteen-year-old ex-Rabble Motor Services Leyland Leopards rebodied with EL2000 bodywork. This view shows before and after it was rebodied.

Twelve months previous Rossendale Blackburn Transport had four nine-year-old ECW-bodied Leyland Tigers rebuilt at the front and rear, using EL2000 parts but with a different front screen.

The 'Atlantean Sprint' was introduced at the request of Southampton Citybus. Based on the EL2000 design, the rear-mounted engine was incorporated into the body, thus eliminating the familiar Leyland Atlantean bustle. Five were built in 1991. Southampton loaned two to Brighton Bus for park and ride duties.

Skills of Nottingham had this fifteen-year-old Volvo B58 rebodied as a double-deck in 1993. The operator claimed that this was the only right-hand B58 to be fitted with a double-deck body.

Launched in 1996, the 'Spryte' was designed by John Worker. Initially on the Dennis Dart SLF, it was available in three lengths up to 10.9 metres and two widths, 2.3 and 2.47 metres. It was built using Alusuisse bolted construction. The first one for Rossendale, to be registered 106 (N106 LCK), is seen here in the Walmersley district of Bury.

Black Prince of Morley Leeds had an EL2000 body fitted to this fifteen-year-old Volvo B58 chassis.

The underfloor Volvo Citybus would become Nottingham's preferred choice in the 1980s. The first two came in 1983. 398 (A39 8CRA) is seen in King Street in the city centre.

Warrington Borough Transport bought both the Leyland Olympian and the Dennis Dominator. 48 (A748 GFY) is here outside Halton bus garage.

Eastbourne Coaches had two Olympian ONLXCT/2Rs on the London service.

The borough of Ipswich had this Leyland Olympian, new in 1985. They also purchased a similarly bodied Dennis Dominator in the same year.

The first order for Alexander-style bodywork was on a batch of fifteen Dennis Dominators for South Yorkshire PTE in 1984. This style was to be named 'E' type, as opposed to the Alexander 'R' type.

Hyndburn was also converted to the Dennis Dominator, taking nine between 1979 and 1985. Most if not all were sold to Chester.

In 1992 Grey-Green Coaches said it could save £500,000 by converting sixteen surplus eight-year-old Volvo B10M coaches to service buses. The coaches were stripped by East Lancs and refurbished, which included low profile wheels and tyres. The nine doubles and seven single-deckers ended up 1.7 metres shorter than the original 12-metre coaches, which produced no rear overhang. This is the first double-deck.

One from the same batch of buses (above) that ended up with Thornes of Budwith. Note the short rear overhang.

Kettlewell of Retford took two Dodge 50s in 1987. A total of thirty-five Dodge minibuses were built and sold by the company.

Two Volvo B10M-56 double-deck coaches went to Great Yarmouth in 1987.

In the year 2000 the Go-Ahead Group took forty-seven double-deck Tridents. Twenty went to Brighton & Hove and the remaining twenty-seven went to Go North East. One of the latter examples is seen here in Gateshead when new.

Rossendale Transport bought only one new Leyland Olympian, which came in April 1987, seen here in Bury when new. It was withdrawn in 1995.

The only new double-deck Scania to enter service in 1993 was this example for Maynes of Manchester. It is photographed on its first outing on Sunday 1 August on the 460 service to Matlock.

Two of the 1988 delivery of Volvo Citybuses to Nottingham City Transport.

Blackpool Transport took six Leyland Olympians in April 1989. 368 (F368 AFR) is on the 22 service to St Annes Square.

Eight single-deck Scania N113DRB were supplied to Kingston upon Hull in 1989. When new the purchase price was just over £72,000 per bus, a far cry from the price of a similar bus today.

At a special handover ceremony in Hull on 10 July, Arthur Danson is seen in the middle of the photograph shaking the hand of the transport committee chairman.

Twenty-four Lowlanders on the DAF 250LF were supplied to Arriva in 2001, fifteen for Fox County and nine for Northumbria. 7436 (Y686 EBR) is a Fox County example before delivery.

Six Dennis Dominators were ordered by Warrington Borough Transport for delivery in 1988. Two of the order were for its 'Coachlines' operations. They seated seventy-six, and were equipped with ABS brakes. During its nineteen-year production run Dennis built 1,001 Dominator chassis. Incidentally East Lancs bodied the first example, as well as the last one.

Rossendale Transport's first new full-size single-deckers for fourteen years came in March 1989: four Leyland Tigers. Three were fitted with fifty-one bus seats, and the fourth to dual-purpose specification and forty-nine seats.

Ten Dennis Dominators went to North Western in June 1989. Their slogan at the time was 'A new kind of service from a different kind of bus company'.

The final Leyland Lions, and the first with East Lancs bodywork, went to Nottingham. Five were eighty-eight-seat service buses, and the other five, one of which is seen on Long Row East in January 1989, are in this special 'Harrods' livery.

One of the eighty-eight seaters, 388 (F388 GVO) at Strelley in Nottingham.

The Volvo Citybus was also delivered to North Western during 1989/90. In March 1988 the National Bus Company (NBC) sold the North Western Road Car Company to the Drawlane Group, which in 1992 was restructured as British Bus. Also in 1992 British Bus was acquired by the Cowie Group, which five years later became Arriva.

A new customer in 1993 was Ralph Bullock of Cheadle Cheshire, who had two of some of the last Leyland Olympian chassis to be built. L10 BUL is here in Stockport bus station on the 42 to Manchester.

Yet another new customer was Thamesdown Transport Ltd. Five Dennis Dominators with Gardner 6LXCT engines and Voith gearboxes came at the end of 1990. This one is shown here at Showbus.

A line-up of three Midland Red North buses. On the left is a low-height Dennis Dominator, a rebodied Leyland Tiger and a Dennis Dart.

Four Dennis Dominators went to Grimsby-Cleethorpes in May 1991. Grimsby's previous Dominators had bodywork by Walter Alexander.

Leicester CityBus was a big Dennis fan. In 1991 they had some 123 Dennis Dominators, the majority with East Lancs bodywork. So in 1991 when it needed new single-deck buses the Dennis Falcon was the obvious choice. Six came in 1991/2. However, the next order for Falcons had bodywork by Northern Counties of Wigan.

The Dennis Dominator was becoming ever more popular. Bournemouth was the latest recipient, taking seven in August 1990.

The thirty-six two-door Volvo Citybuses delivered to London & Country in 1990/91 were specified with a shorter rear overhang to improve manoeuvrability in central London. They were bought specifically for two tender gained routes: the 78 Forest–Shoreditch and the 176 Penge–Oxford Circus.

Here at Trafalgar Square we see a new grey-green Volvo B10M, 917 (H917 XYT), being passed by London & Country Volvo Citybus D10M 654 (H654 GPF).

Plymouth's two Volvo Citybus D10Ms of 1991 had seventy-eight Vogel seats and a walk-in rear luggage compartment. Inside they had open-mesh coat racks on both decks.

Dennis's Coaches of Dukinfield, Cheshire, ordered three Dennis Tridents in 2000. W531 GCW was the only one painted in the red and yellow livery. The bus was collected from Blackburn at 10 a.m., and by 2 p.m. the same day it was in service in Manchester.

Dennis's Coaches had two more Tridents in October 2000. These latest buses carried a new version of the previous livery, grey instead of yellow, to avoid confusion with First Pennine.

Blackburn Transport took five dual-purpose Volvo B10Ms, fitted with fifty-one-seat EL2000 bodywork. These were the first UK B10Ms to be fitted with the Allison MT467 automatic gearbox. They were initially used on the Clitheroe to Manchester service.

The three Dennis Dominators that Maynes of Manchester obtained in March 1993 had been ordered and built for Strathclyde. They were cancelled by the Glasgow operator before delivery. Maynes was offered them and took delivery four weeks later.

One of the four Scania N113CRBs with EL2000 bodywork supplied to Tayside in 1993.

Blue Bus of Horwich, near Bolton, took an EL2000-bodied Dennis Dart in 1993, which had an appropriate BLU registration.

Blue Bus also further upgraded its fleet with its first new double-deck purchase in the shape of three Pyoneer-bodied Volvo Olympians. R44 BLU is seen here at Freeport Fleetwood on the X1 service.

Two Volvo B72Ls, part of an order for thirty-six for London General, here at Morden underground station in 2002.

Yorkshire Traction bought their first new double-decks for sixteen years, two of which with Myllennium Vyking bodywork. 906 (YM02 CLZ) is on the X32 Leeds–Barnsley–Sheffield service at the Meadowhall Interchange in July 2002.

Five Dennis Tridents went to Blackburn Transport in 2002, which were 11.4 metres long and had ninety seats. Blackburn's previous Dennis double-decks had been five Dominators in 1981. 3 (PN52 XKH) is here at Darwen Circus.

The Myllennium style of double-deck bodywork was launched in the summer of 2001. The first ones went to the Isle of Mann mounted on ten low-floor DAF DB250 chassis.

Blackpool Transport took nine Dennis Tridents in 2002. 305 (PJ02 PYL) is on Market Street in the company of Leyland Atlantean AN68 350 (GHG 350W).

In 2002 Scania announced it would be offering its first low-floor double-deck chassis to be built in conjunction with East Lancashire Coachbuilders. It would be made available in both 10.5 and 12 metre lengths. The chassis would shipped in kit form and put together at Lancashire Product Developments (LPD) in Leyland. They named it OmniDekka. The first orders came from Nottingham, Brighton & Hove and Metrobus. Metrobus was the first operator to put them on in service. 451 (YU52 XVK) is seen in Croydon soon after delivery in 2003.

Brighton & Hove was the next major operator to receive the OmniDekkas, taking eighteen in 2004. Brighton amassed over a hundred by the time production ended.

Nottingham took the 12-metre version. The first examples arrived in 2003 in the blue version of the Go2 branding. During the eight-year production run Nottingham bought close to 150, thus making it by far the biggest operator of the Scania-East Lancs OmniDekka.

New open-top double-deck buses started to become popular from the late 1990s, and East Lancs capitalised on that growing market. Dualways of Rathcool in Dublin took the Volvo B7TL in 2005, with a 2007 Visionaire B9TL behind.

Unilink Southampton had this OmniDekka serving the airport, university and city centre. At that time (2004) the vehicles on these services were owned by Accord Operations Ltd in Chichester.

In 2004 Bus Eireann took three Volvo B7TL for their Black Ash park and ride service in Cork Eire. DD33 (04-C-12281) is crossing the River Lee in Cork city centre.

The 2004 delivery of Dennis Tridents to Blackpool consisted of six for Line 11 Grange Park to Lytham Saltcoates Road with turquoise livery. A seventh Trident came in the pool black and yellow livery.

In 2004 Lothian Buses had this OmniDekka demonstrator on trial: 999 (SN04 CPE). It was painted in harlequin livery. It is seen on route 37 to Penicuik. Its stay in Edinburgh was short, and in the end Lothian decided to buy the Polish-built Omnicity double-deck.

Ralph Bullock's two OmniDekkas entered service in March 2004 on the 157 Woodford to Manchester Piccadilly. MX04 MYY is picking up passengers in Cheadle town centre, not far from the company's depot.

Quantock Motor Services in Somerset had this half open-top Omnidekka. It was painted in this retro Ribble 'White Lady' livery.

In 2006 they built the Esteem bodywork on a Scania N230UB chassis as a demonstrator. It was eventually sold to Centrebus for use in Leicester.

Arriva Yorkshire DAF DB250 1607 (YJ06 WML) is at Mirfield on the 203 service between Leeds and Hudderfield.

Stagecoach had ten Kinetec MAN 18.240 HOCL-NL (A69), which was basically an Esteem with the MAN Lion City front. 22508 (SF56 FKL) is photographed here on the Ayr–Girvan–Stranraer service.

The only Kinetec double-deck was mounted on the MAN ND283F (A48) chassis. It was built to low height (4 metres), bought by Reading, and painted in the green livery of route 9. A 4.3-metre-high version was planned for London, but was never built.

The first operator for the new Visionaire open-top double-deck was Dublin sightseeing operator Dualways. It was first operated as such on 16 May 2007. It had a covered front section, separated by a glazed partition, and was mounted on a Volvo B9TL chassis.

Arriva's the Original Tour took ten Visionaire Volvo B9TLs in May 2007. VLE 620 (LJ07 UDD) is seen approaching Trafalgar Square.

Tri-axle Dennis Trident belonging to Citybus Hong Kong on the E11 service, 8 February 1999.

Blue Bus had four Myllennium-bodied MAN 14.220s in 2003.

In 2004 Maynes bought two of these Scania N94UB OmniTowns.

Uno Bus, formally University Bus, is operated by the University of Hertfordshire, serving the general public, plus its own students and staff. Three OmniDekkas arrived in 2005. 203 (UH55 UNO) is here at Showbus in Duxford.

Cumbria County Council invested £475,000 on three Dennis Tridents that were to be operated on their behalf by Stagecoach on the X35 service between Kendal and Barrow-in-Furness. The buses were funded by the government's Rural Challenge Scheme.

Reading's intake of new buses in 2006 consisted of seventeen 10.7-metre-long OmniDekkas. They were bought for the 25 and 26 group of services to Calcot–Southcote–City Centre.

Brighton & Hove was the second largest operator (after Nottingham) of the Scania OmniDekka. 671 (YN07 UOT) is part of the last batch to be delivered to B&H in 2007.

In the summer of 2007 Transdev London United took nine Scania N230UDs with the Olympus bodywork. S09 (YN07 LHZ) is passing through Parliament Square.

Metroline ordered thirty-three Olympus Scanias. Only around half that total had been to London before the end of the East Lancashire Coachbuilders name on 17 August 2007. The first one in service was SEL LK07 AZX, seen at Acton in July 2007.

This Leyland Titan PD3A/1 was supplied to Leicester City Transport in 1964. It has now been fully restored and is seen here at Showbus in 2014.